JUMPIN' JIM'S™

Ukulele Christmas

Compiled and Arranged by Jim Beloff

HAL•LEONARD®
CORPORATION
7777 W. BLUEMOUND RD. P.O. BOX 13819 MILWAUKEE, WI 53213

Edited by Ronny S. Schiff
Cover and Art Direction by Elizabeth Maihock Beloff
Graphics and Music Typography by Charylu Roberts
Vintage Christmas Postcards from Flea Markets

FOREWORD

This book has a special meaning for me. Like almost everyone else, I happen to love the holiday season. As a boy growing up in Connecticut, I remember looking forward to seeing neighbors putting up their Christmas lights, local merchants decorating their stores and my entire hometown putting on its holiday face.

Of course, I've always loved Christmas carols. Every year these classic melodies get trotted out and every year I am reminded of how enduring and indestructible they are. In fact, the "cold turkey" on December 26th can refer not only to the leftovers from the day before, but also that quite suddenly these songs are yanked away from us until the following year.

Part of my particular affection for the Christmas season also has to do with the fact that December 25th is my birthday. As you'll see in my song "When You're Born on Christmas Day," I enjoyed having my birthday at such a musical time. Nowadays, though, my birthday usually includes me playing uke to accompany the songs in this book. In preparing these arrangements, I was once again delighted at how well the humble ukulele can serve a wide variety of music. A good example of that is the chord solo for the classical piece, "Dance of the Sugar-Plum Fairy," from Tchaikovsky's *The Nutcracker Suite*. Here's hoping that the uke can bring a lot of smiles to your holidays!

Many thanks to all the elves who helped put this together. In particular, Charylu Roberts, Wendy DeWitt, Peter Wingerd, Fred Sokolow, Ronny Schiff and everyone at Hal Leonard. Finally, Happy Birthday and Merry Christmas to Liz who, as a December 23rd birthday baby, understands!

—*Jumpin' Jim*

HOW TO USE THIS BOOK

Parenthetical Chords

Throughout this book you will find chords (or chord groups) in parentheses (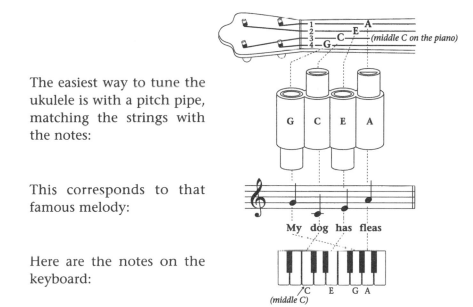Dm). These "parenthetical" chords are there to provide a more challenging arrangement for experienced players. For those who are less experienced, you may want to ignore these chords until you feel more confident.

Tuning

The smallest and most popular size of the ukulele is the soprano. All of the songs in this book were arranged for the soprano ukulele in C tuning. Nonetheless, if you tune any sized uke as shown below, you will be able to play the chords as written.

The easiest way to tune the ukulele is with a pitch pipe, matching the strings with the notes:

This corresponds to that famous melody:

Here are the notes on the keyboard:

Transposing

If any song feels too high or too low for you to sing comfortably, you may want to change its key. To do this it is necessary to change all the chords. Use the chart below that shows you the key and the related chords:

	Major			Minor		
Chords in C:	C	F	G7	Am	Dm	E7
D♭:	D♭	G♭	A♭7	D♭m	E♭m	F7
D:	D	G	A7	Bm	Em	F#7
E♭:	E♭	A♭	B♭7	Cm	Fm	G7
E:	E	A	B7	C#m	F#m	G#7
F:	F	B♭	C7	Dm	Gm	A7
G♭:	G♭	C♭	D♭7	E♭m	A♭m	B♭7
G:	G	C	D7	Em	Am	B7
A♭:	A♭	D♭	E♭7	Fm	B♭m	C7
A:	A	D	E7	F#m	Bm	C#7
B♭:	B♭	E♭	F7	Gm	Cm	D7
B:	B	E	F#7	G#m	C#m	D#7

Strums

The songs do not indicate strums or rhythm markings. If you're looking for basic strumming suggestions, refer to *Jumpin' Jim's Ukulele Tips 'n' Tunes*.

CHORD CHART

Tune Ukulele

G   C   E   A

MAJOR CHORDS

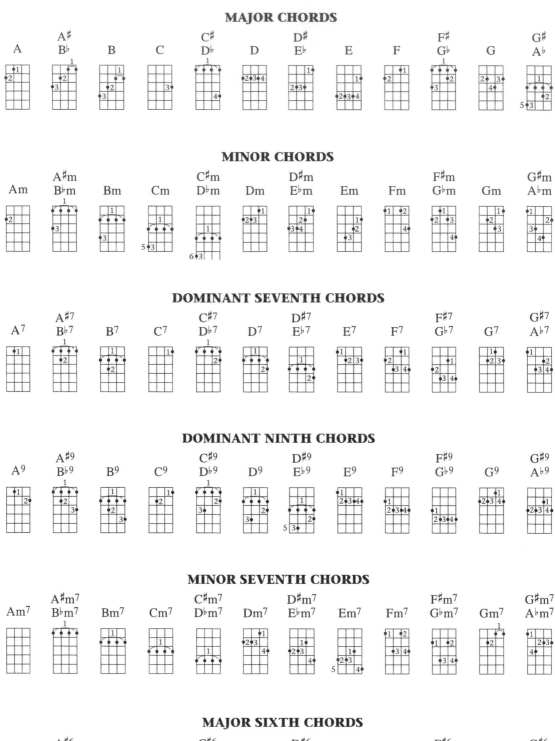

MINOR CHORDS

DOMINANT SEVENTH CHORDS

DOMINANT NINTH CHORDS

MINOR SEVENTH CHORDS

MAJOR SIXTH CHORDS

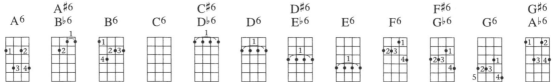

MINOR SIXTH CHORDS

Am6	A#m6 / B♭m6	Bm6	Cm6	C#m6 / D♭m6	Dm6	D#m6 / E♭m6	Em6	Fm6	F#m6 / G♭m6	Gm6	G#m6 / A♭m6

MAJOR SEVENTH CHORDS

Amaj7	A#maj7 / B♭maj7	Bmaj7	Cmaj7	C#maj7 / D♭maj7	Dmaj7	D#maj7 / E♭maj7	Emaj7	Fmaj7	F#maj7 / G♭maj7	Gmaj7	G#maj7 / A♭maj7

DOMINANT SEVENTH CHORDS WITH RAISED FIFTH (7th+5)

A7+5	A#7+5 / B♭7+5	B7+5	C7+5	C#7+5 / D♭7+5	D7+5	D#7+5 / E♭7+5	E7+5	F7+5	F#7+5 / G♭7+5	G7+5	G#7+5 / A♭7+5

DOMINANT SEVENTH CHORDS WITH LOWERED FIFTH (7th-5)

A7-5	A#7-5 / B♭7-5	B7-5	C7-5	C#7-5 / D♭7-5	D7-5	D#7-5 / E♭7-5	E7-5	F7-5	F#7-5 / G♭7-5	G7-5	G#7-5 / A♭7-5

AUGMENTED FIFTH CHORDS (aug or +)

Aaug	A#aug / B♭aug	Baug	Caug	C#aug / D♭aug	Daug	D#aug / E♭aug	Eaug	Faug	F#aug / G♭aug	Gaug	G#aug / A♭aug

DIMINISHED SEVENTH CHORDS (dim)

Adim	A#dim / B♭dim	Bdim	Cdim	C#dim / D♭dim	Ddim	D#dim / E♭dim	Edim	Fdim	F#dim / G♭dim	Gdim	G#dim / A♭dim

Angels We Have Heard On High

Traditional

Old French Carol

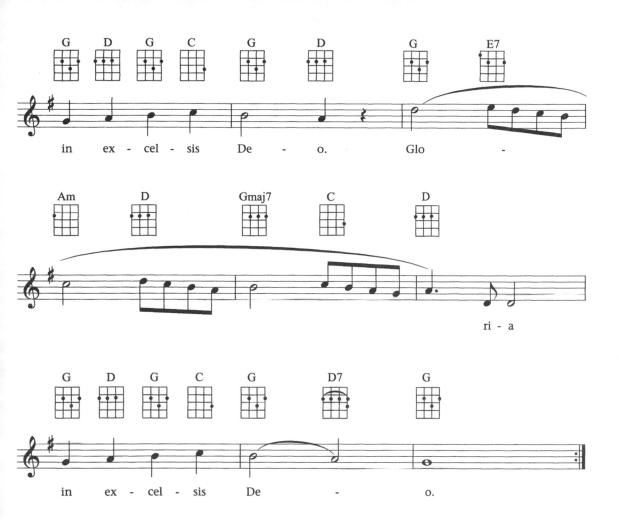

in ex - cel - sis De - o. Glo - ri - a in ex - cel - sis De - o.

3. Come to Bethlehem and see
   Him whose birth the angels sing.
   Come, adore on bended knee,
   Christ, the Lord, our new-born King.
   Gloria in excelsis Deo,
   Gloria in excelsis Deo.

4. See Him in a manger laid,
   whom the choir of angels praise.
   Mary, Joseph, lend your aid,
   while our hearts in love we raise.
   Gloria in excelsis Deo,
   Gloria in excelsis Deo.

CHRISTMAS GREETINGS
May the joy of the day
from its very start
take full possession of
all your heart

Auld Lang Syne

Words by ROBERT BURNS

Old Scottish Melody

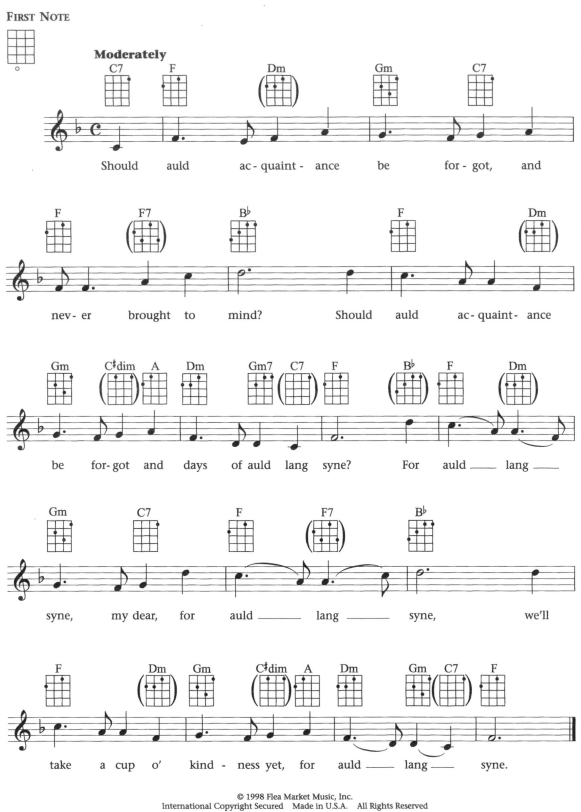

Away in a Manger

Music by
JAMES R. MURRAY

FIRST NOTE

Tenderly

1. A - way in a man - ger, no crib for His
2. The cat - tle are low - ing, the poor ba - by

bed, the lit - tle Lord Je - sus lay down his sweet
wakes, but lit - tle Lord Je - sus, no cry - ing He

head. The stars in the sky _____ looked down where He
makes; I love Thee, Lord Je - sus, look down from the

lay, the lit - tle Lord Je - sus, a - sleep on the hay.
sky, and stay by my cra - dle 'til morn - ing is nigh.

3. Be near me, Lord Jesus,
I ask Thee to stay
close by me forever
and love me, I pray.
Bless all the dear children
in Thy tender care,
and take us to heaven
to live with Thee there.

Bring a Torch, Jeannette, Isabella

Translated by
EDWARD CUTHBERT NUNN

French Traditional Carol

2. It is wrong when the Child is sleeping,
it is wrong to talk so loud.
Silence, all, as you gather around,
lest your noise should waken Jesus.
Hush! hush! see how fast He slumbers;
hush! hush! see how fast He sleeps!

3. Softly to the little stable,
softly for a moment come.
Look and see how charming is Jesus,
how He is warm. His cheeks are rosy!
Hush! hush! see how the Child is sleeping;
hush! hush! see how He smiles in dreams!

The Coventry Carol

Words by
ROBERT CROO

Sixteenth Century
English Melody

FIRST NOTE

Tenderly

1. Lul - lay, thou lit - tle ti - ny child,
2. O sis - ters too, how may we do,

by by, lul - ly lul - lay. _____ Lul -
for to pre - serve this day? _____ This

lay, thou lit - tle ti - ny child.
poor young - ling for whom we sing.

By by, lul - ly, lul - lay. _____
By by, lul - ly, lul - lay. _____

3. Herod, the king,
   in his raging
   charged he hath this day.
   his men of might,
   in his own sight,
   all young children to slay.

4. That woe is me,
   poor child for thee!
   And ever morn and day,
   for thy parting
   neither say nor sing.
   By by, lully lullay!

Dance of the Sugar-Plum Fairy

Music by
PETER I. TCHAIKOVSKY

Delicately

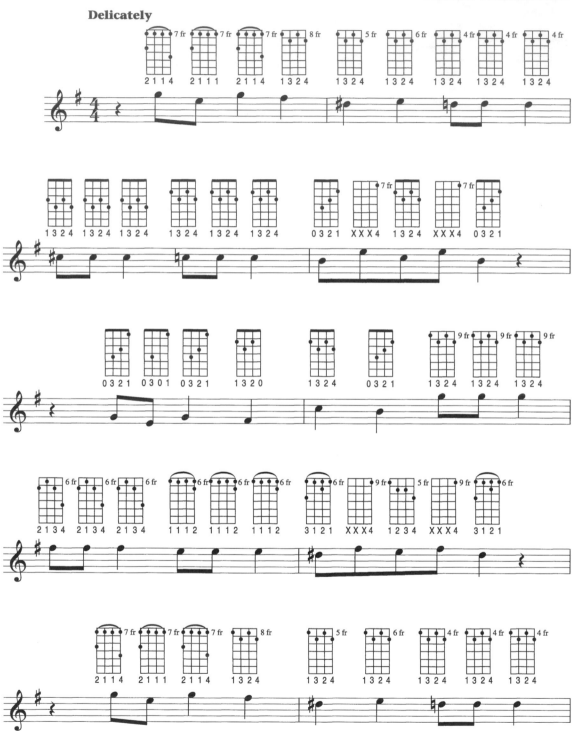

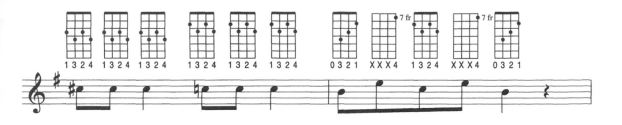

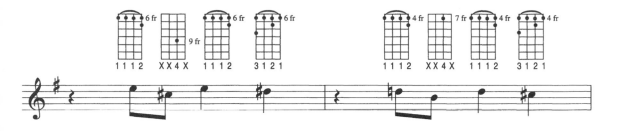

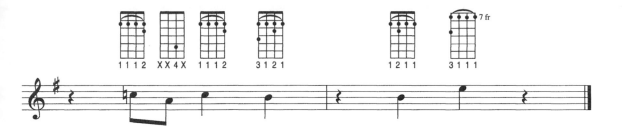

Deck the Halls

Old Welsh Air

FIRST NOTE

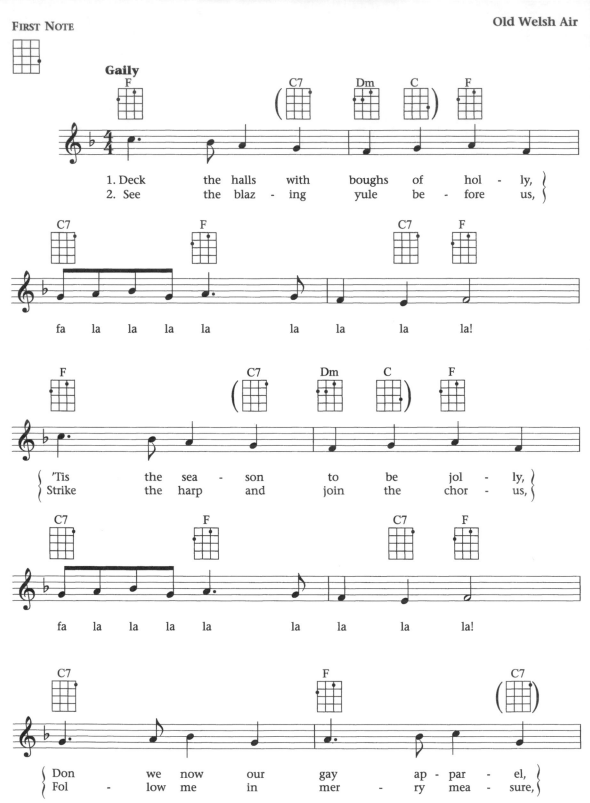

Gaily

1. Deck the halls with boughs of hol - ly,
2. See the blaz - ing yule be - fore us,

fa la la la la la la la la!

'Tis the sea - son to be jol - ly,
Strike the harp and join the chor - us,

fa la la la la la la la la!

Don we now our gay ap - par - el,
Fol - low me in mer - ry mea - sure,

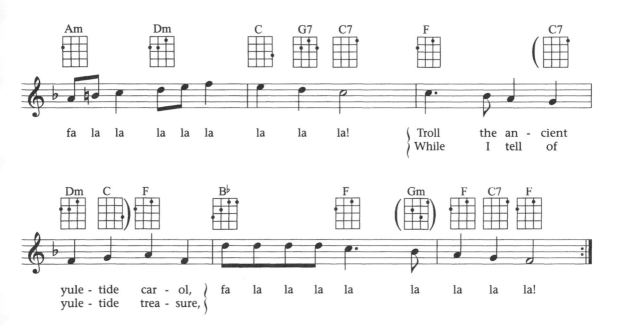

fa la la   la la la   la la   la!

{ Troll   the an - cient
{ While   I tell of

yule - tide   car - ol, { fa la la la la   la la la   la!
yule - tide   trea - sure, {

3. Fast away the old year passes,
   fa la la la la la la la la!
   Hail the new, ye lads and lasses,
   fa la la la la la la la la!
   Sing we joyous all together,
   fal la la la la la la la la!
   Heedless of the wind and weather,
   fa la la la la la la la la!

The First Nowell

English Traditional Carol

FIRST NOTE

Moderately Slow

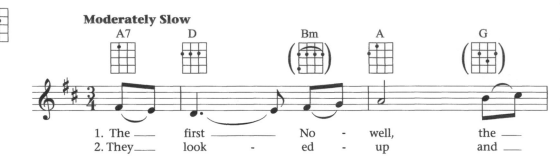

1. The ___ first ___ No - well, the ___
2. They ___ look - ed - up and ___

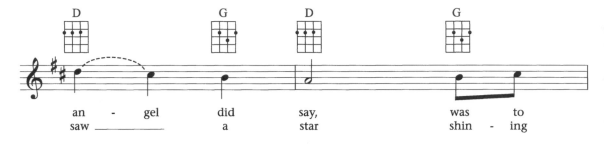

an - gel did say, was to
saw ___ a star shin - ing

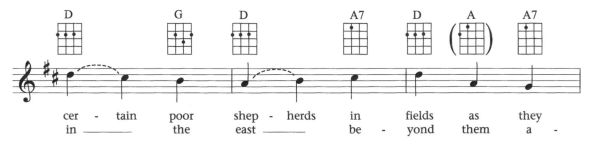

cer - tain poor shep - herds in fields as they
in ___ the east ___ be - yond them a -

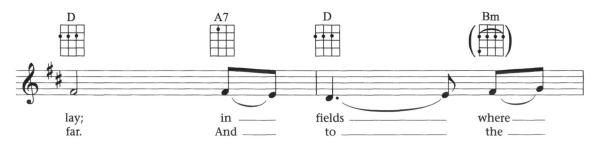

lay; in ___ fields ___ where ___
far. And ___ to ___ the ___

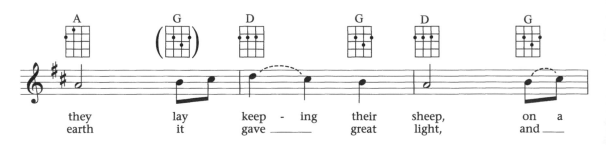

they lay keep - ing their sheep, on a
earth it gave ___ great light, and ___

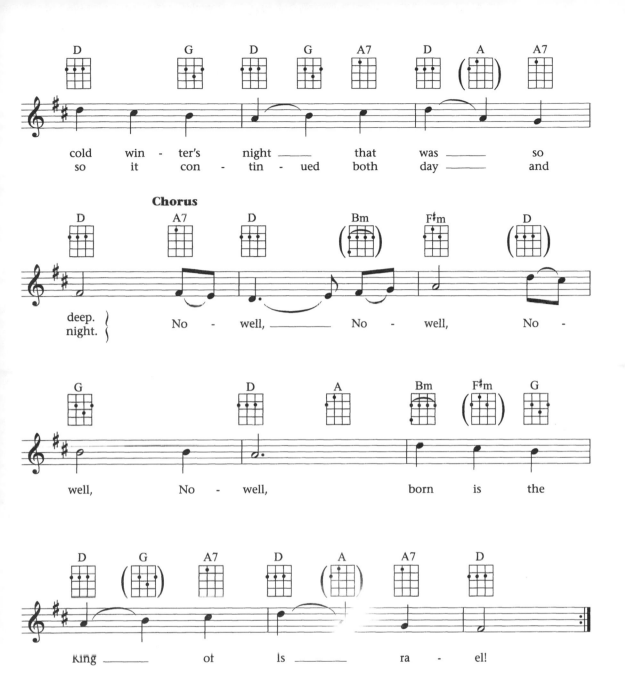

cold win - ter's night _____ that was _____ so
so it con - tin - ued both day _____ and

Chorus

deep. } No - well, _____ No - well, No -
night. }

well, No - well, born is the

King _____ of Is _____ ra - el!

3. And by the light of that same star,
   three wise men came from country far;
   to seek for a King was their intent,
   and to follow the star wherever it went.
   (Chorus)

4. This star drew nigh to the northwest,
   over Bethlehem it took its rest,
   and there it did both stop and stay,
   right over the place where Jesus lay.
   (Chorus)

5. Then entered in those wise men three,
   full reverently upon the knee,
   and offered there, in His presence,
   their gold, and myrrh, and frankincense.
   (Chorus)

6. Then let us all, with one accord,
   sing praise to our Heavenly Lord,
   that hath made heaven and earth of nought,
   and with His blood mankind hath bought.
   (Chorus)

God Rest Ye Merry, Gentlemen

English Traditional
Melody

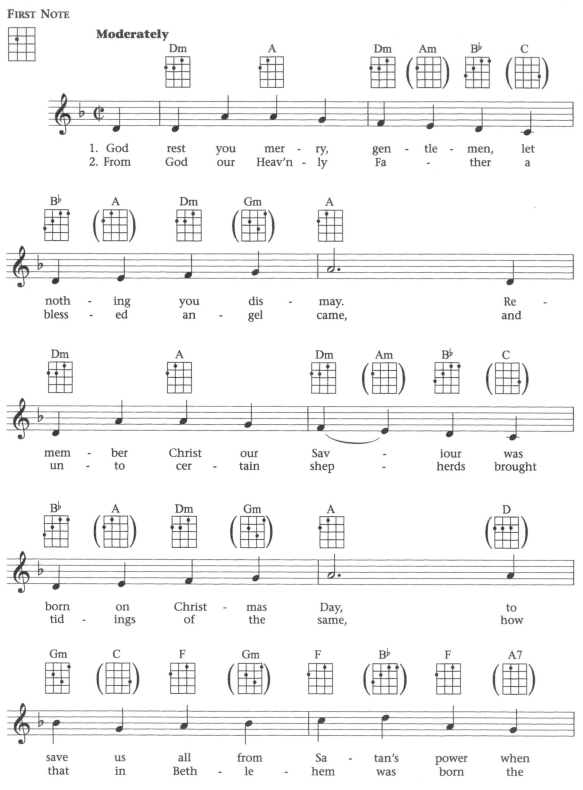

1. God rest you mer - ry, gen - tle - men, let noth - ing you dis - may. Re -
2. From God our Heav'n - ly Fa - ther a bless - ed an - gel came, and

mem - ber Christ our Sav - iour was born on Christ - mas Day,
un - to cer - tain shep - herds was brought tid - ings of the same,

to save us all from Sa - tan's power when
how that in Beth - le - hem was born the

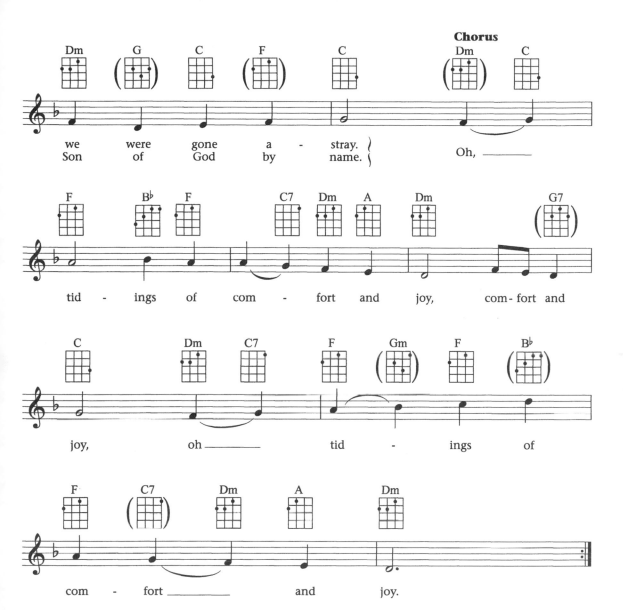

Chorus

we were gone a - stray.
Son of God by name.

Oh, ——

tid - ings of com - fort and joy, com-fort and

joy, oh ———— tid - ings of

com - fort ———— and joy.

3. In Bethlehem, in Jewry
   this blessed Babe was born,
   and laid within a manger
   upon this holy morn.
   To which his Mother Mary
   did nothing take in scorn.
   (Chorus)

4. "Fear not then," said the Angel,
   "Let nothing you affright,
   this day is born a Savior
   of a pure Vigin bright,
   to free all those who trust in Him
   from Satan's power and might."
   (Chorus)

5. The shepherds at those tidings
   rejoiced much in mind.
   And left their flocks a-feeding,
   in tempest, storm, and wind.
   And went to Bethlehem straightway,
   this Blessed Babe to find.
   (Chorus)

6. But when to Bethlehem they came,
   whereat this infant lay,
   they found Him in a manger,
   Where oxen feed on hay.
   His Mother Mary kneeling down,
   unto the Lord did pray.
   (Chorus)

7. Now to the Lord sing praises,
   All you within this place,
   And with true love and brotherhood
   each other new embrace;
   this holy tide of Christmas
   all others doth deface.
   (Chorus)

Good King Wenceslas

Words by
JOHN MASON NEALE

Traditional

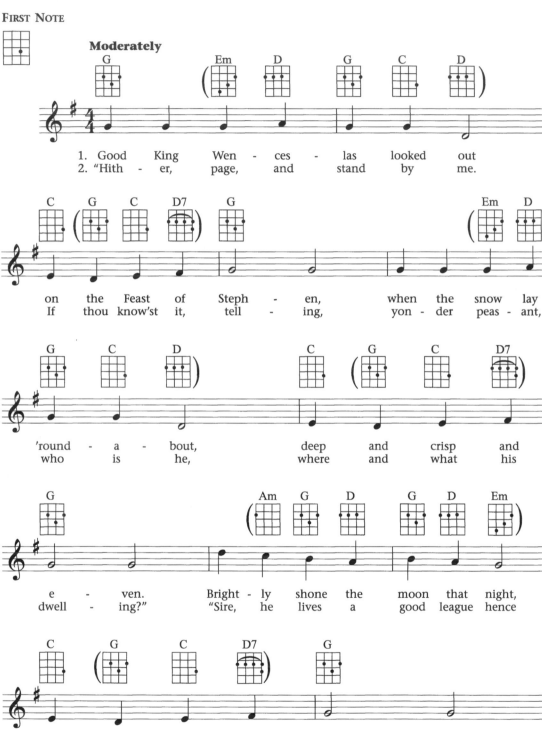

1. Good King Wen - ces - las looked out
2. "Hith - er, page, and stand by me.

on the Feast of Steph - en, when the snow lay
If thou know'st it, tell - ing, yon - der peas - ant,

'round - a - bout, deep and crisp and
who is he, where and what and his

e - ven. Bright - ly shone the moon that night,
dwell - ing?" "Sire, he lives a good league hence

though the frost was cru - el,
un - der - neath the moun - tain;

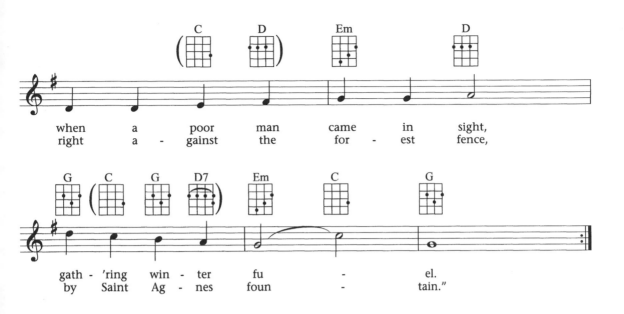

when   a   poor   man   came   in   sight,
right   a - gainst   the   for - est   fence,

gath - 'ring   win - ter   fu   -   el.
by   Saint   Ag - nes   foun   -   tain."

3. "Bring me flesh, and bring me wine,
    bring me pinelogs hither;
    thou and I well see him dine
    when we bear them thither."
    Page and monarch forth they went,
    forth they went together,
    through the rude wind's wild lament
    and the bitter weather.

4. "Sire, the night is darker now,
    and the wind blows stronger;
    fails my heart, I know not how,
    I can go no longer."
    "Mark my footsteps, my good page.
    Tread thou in them boldly,
    thou shalt find the winter's rage
    freeze thy blood less coldly!"

5. In his master's steps he trod,
    where the snow lay dinted;
    heat was in the very sod,
    which the saint had printed.
    Therefore, Christian men, be sure,
    wealth or rank possessing,
    ye who now will bless the poor,
    shall yourselves find blessing.

Go Tell It on the Mountain

Spiritual

1. When I was a learn - er, I
2. He made me a watch - man up -

sought both night and day; I
on the cit - y wall, and

asked the Lord to aid me, and
if I am a Chris - tian, I

He showed me the way. _____
am the least of all. _____

Go tell it on the

moun - tain, o - ver the hills and

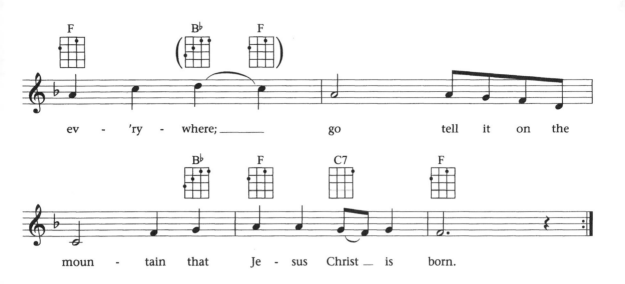

ev - 'ry - where; _____ go tell it on the

moun - tain that Je - sus Christ _ is born.

3. While shepherds kept their watching,
   o'er wand'ring flock by night…
   Behold! From out the Heavens,
   there shown a holy light.

4. And lo, when they had seen it,
   they all bowed down and prayed.
   Then they travelled on together,
   to where the Babe was laid.

Hark! The Herald Angels Sing

Words by
CHARLES WESLEY

Music by
FELIX MENDELSSOHN

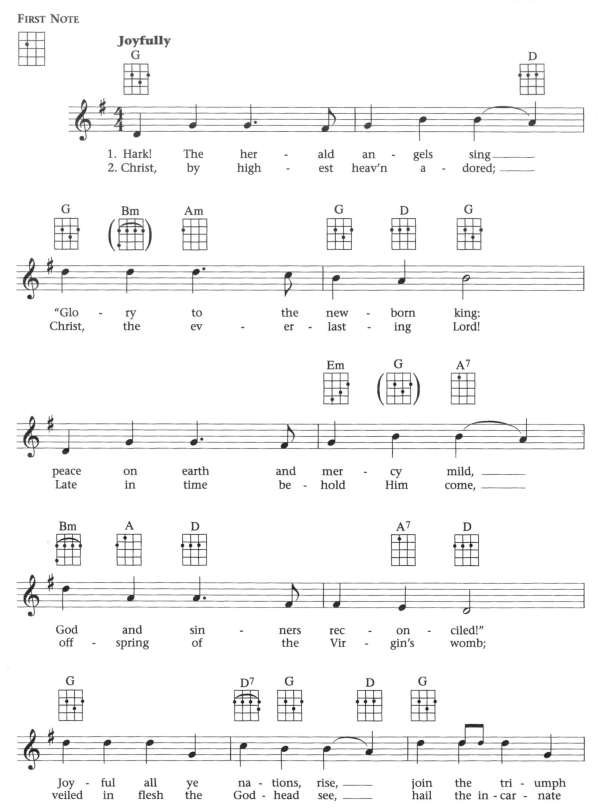

of   the   skies; ———   with   the   an - gel - ic
de - i - ty, ———   pleased   as   man   with

host   pro - claim,   "Christ   is —— born   in
men   to   dwell,   Je - sus —— our   Em -

Beth - le - hem!"   {   Hark!   The her - ald   an - gels   sing:
man - u - el.   }

"Glo - ry —— to   the   new - born   King"

3. Hail the heaven-born Prince of Peace!
   Hail the Sun of Righteousness!
   Light and life to all He brings,
   Risen with healing in His wings.
   Mild He lays His glory by.
   Born that man no more may die,
   born to raise the sons of earth,
   born to give them second birth.
   Hark! the herald angels sing,
   "Glory to the new-born King."

Here We Come A-Wassailing

English Traditional Carol

FIRST NOTE

Gaily

Here we come a - was - sail - ing a -
We are not dai - ly beg - gars that

mong the leaves so green.
beg from door to door,

Here we come a - wan - d'ring, so
but we are neigh - bor's chil - dren whom

fair _____ to be seen.
you have seen be fore:

Chorus

Love and

joy come to you, and to you your was - sail

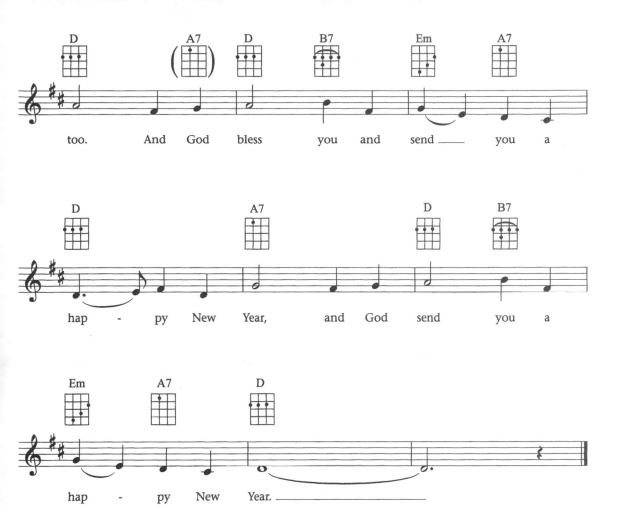

too. And God bless you and send ____ you a

hap - py New Year, and God send you a

hap - py New Year. ____

3. Good Master and good Mistress,
   as you sit by the fire,
   pray think of us poor children,
   who wander in the mire.
   (Chorus)

4. God bless the master of this house,
   likewise the mistress too;
   and all the little children
   that 'round the table go.
   (Chorus)

The Holly and the Ivy

English Traditional Carol

Old French Melody

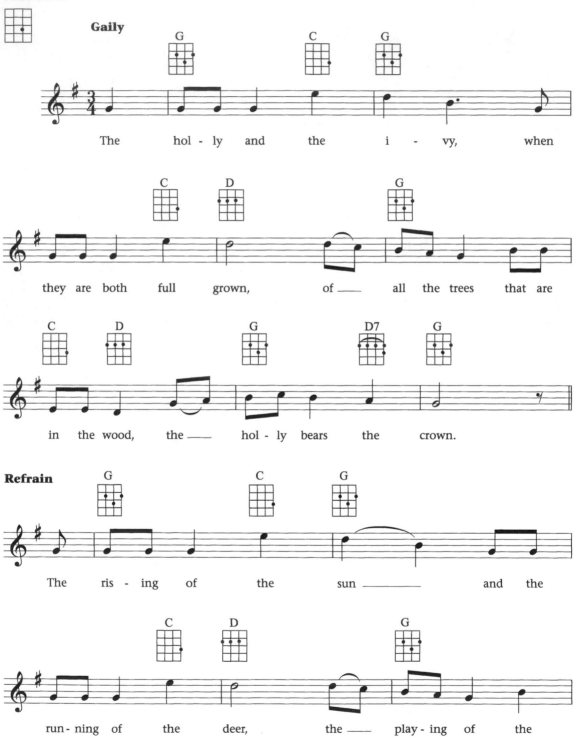

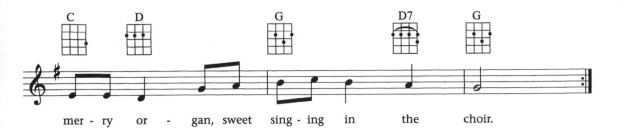

mer - ry   or - gan,   sweet   sing - ing   in   the   choir.

2. The holly bears a blossom,
   as white as lily flower.
   And Mary bore sweet Jesus Christ,
   to be our sweet Savior.
   (Refrain)

3. The holly bears a berry,
   as red as any blood.
   And Mary bore sweet Jesus Christ,
   to do poor sinners good.
   (Refrain)

4. The holly bears a prickle,
   as sharp as any thorn.
   And Mary bore sweet Jesus Christ
   on Christmas Day in the morn.
   (Refrain)

5. The holly bears a bark,
   as bitter as any gall.
   And Mary bore sweet Jesus Christ
   for to redeem us all.
   (Refrain)

6. The holly and the ivy
   now both are full well grown.
   Of all the trees that are in the wood,
   the holly bears the crown.
   (Refrain)

It Came Upon the Midnight Clear

Words by
EDMUND H. SEARS

Music by
RICHARD S. WILLIS

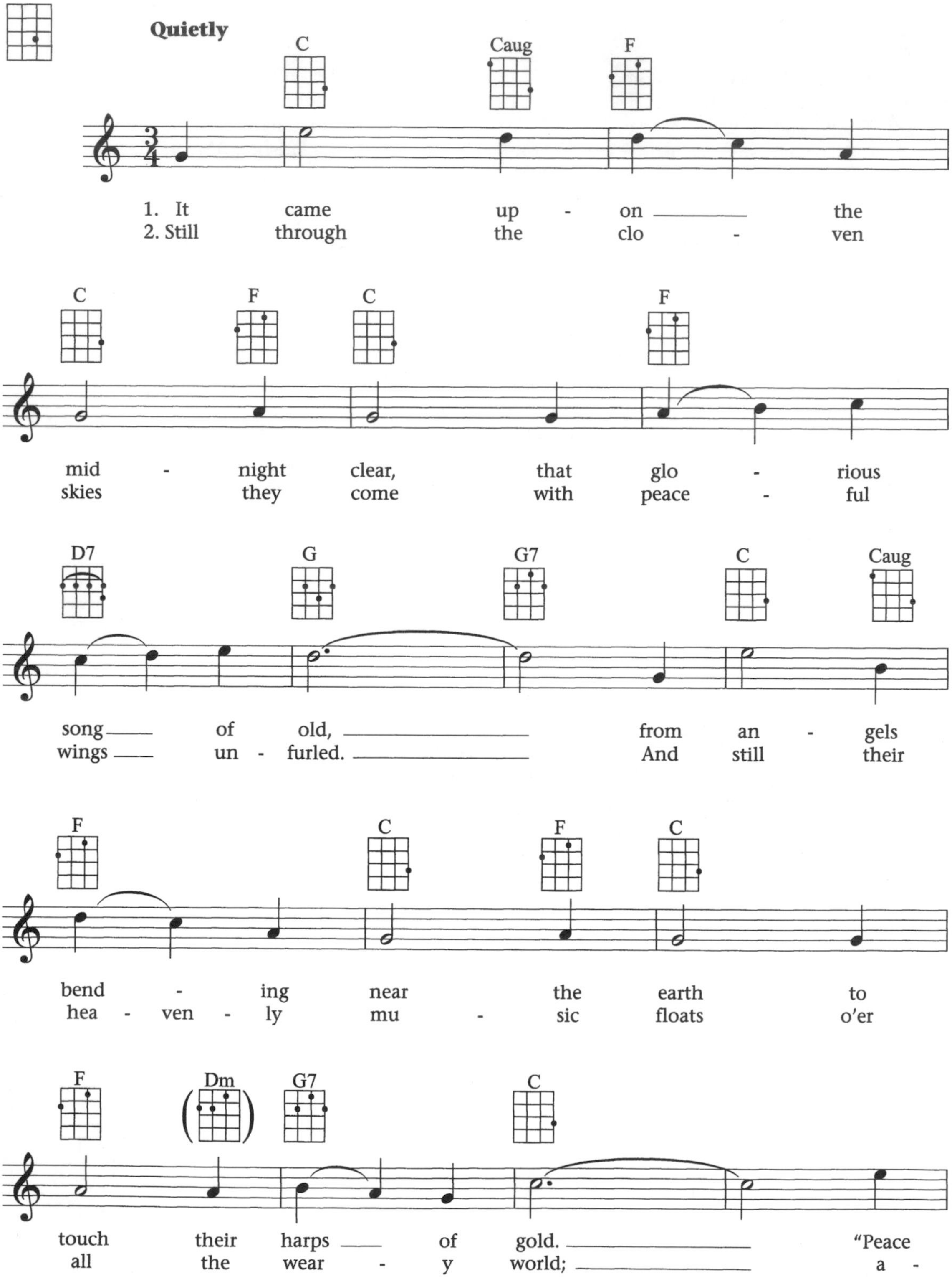

First Note
Quietly
C
Caug
F
1. It came up - on the
2. Still through the clo - ven
C
F
C
F
mid - night clear, that glo - rious
skies they come with peace - ful
D7
G
G7
C
Caug
song of old, from an - gels
wings un - furled. And still their
F
C
F
C
bend - ing near the earth to
hea - ven - ly mu - sic floats o'er
F
(Dm)
G7
C
touch their harps of gold. "Peace
all the wear - y world; a -

on / the / earth, ___ / good / will / to / men, / from
bove / its / sad ___ / and / low - ly / plains / from / they

Heav - en's / all / gra - cious / King." _____ / The
bend ___ / on / hov - er - ing / wing. _____ / And

world / in / sol - emn / still - ness / lay / to
ev - er / o - ver / its / Ba - bel / sounds / the

hear / the / an - gels / sing. _____
bless - ed / an - gels / sing. _____

3. And ye beneath life's crushing load,
   whose forms are bending low,
   who toil along the climbing way
   with painful steps and slow.
   Look now for glad and golden hours,
   come swiftly on the wing.
   O rest beside the weary road
   and hear the angels sing.

4. For lo, the days are hast'ning on,
   by prophet bards foretold.
   When with the ever circling years
   comes 'round the age of gold.
   When peace shall over all the earth
   its ancient splendor fling,
   and the whole world give back the song,
   which now the angels sing.

Jingle Bells

Words and Music by
JAMES PIERPONT

1. Dash-ing through the snow in a one-horse o-pen sleigh,
2. Day or two a-go I thought I'd take a ride, and

o'er the fields we go, laugh-ing all the way;
soon Miss Fan-nie Bright was seat-ed by my side; the

bells on bob-tail ring, mak-ing spir-its bright; what
horse was lean and lank, mis-for-tune seemed his lot, he

fun it is to ride and sing a sleigh-ing song to-night!
got in-to a drift-ed bank and we, we got up-set.

Chorus

Jin - gle bells! Jin - gle bells! Jin - gle all the way!

Oh, what fun it is to ride in a one - horse o - pen sleigh! — one - horse o - pen sleigh!

3. Now the ground is white,
   go it while you're young.
   Take the girls tonight,
   and sing this sleighing song.
   Just get a bobtailed nag,
   two-forty for his speed.
   Then hitch him to an open sleigh,
   and crack you'll take the lead.
          (Chorus)

Jolly Old Saint Nicholas

Traditional

FIRST NOTE

1. Jol - ly old Saint Nich - o - las, lean your ear this
2. When the clock is strik - ing twelve, when I'm fast a -

way! Don't you tell a sin - gle soul
sleep, down the chim - ney broad and black,

what I'm going to say. Christ - mas Eve is com - ing soon;
with your pack you'll creep. All the stock - ings you will find

now, you dear old man, whis - per what you'll
hang - ing in a row; mine will be the

bring to me; tell me if you can.
short - est one, you'll be sure to know.

3. Johnny wants a pair of skates; Suzy wants a sled;
Nellie wants a picture book, yellow, blue and red.
Now I think I'll leave to you what to give the rest.
Choose for me, dear Santa Claus, you will know the best.

Joy to the World

Words by
ISAAC WATTS

Music by
LOWELL MASON
(attributed to G. Handel)

3. No more let sins and sorrows grow,
   nor thorns infest the ground.
   He comes to make His blessings flow
   far as the curse is found.
   Far as the curse is found,
   far as, far as the curse is found.

4. He rules the world with truth and grace,
   and makes the nations prove
   the glories of His righteousness
   and wonders of His love.
   And wonders of His love,
   and wonders, wonders of His love.

The Last House

Music & Lyrics by
JIM BELOFF

FIRST NOTE

1. It's Feb - ru - ar - y now, ___ the hol - i - days have
2. The rain - y sea - son's here, ___ all this week it
3. Al - though I must ad - mit ___ when prob - lems of the
4. It kind of makes me smile, ___ to think they might be

come and gone, ___ but you've still got your Christ - mas ___ lights
poured and poured, ___ I feared for your ex - ten - sion ___ cord.
world in - trude, ___ just see - ing all those pret - ty ___ lights,
there in June, ___ twin - kling 'neath the sum - mer ___ moon.

burn - in' on, ___ burn - in' on. ___   2. Don't you know ___ you've won
helps my mood, ___ my at - ti - tude. ___   4. Please don't take ___ them down

Chorus

___ the a - ward? ___   You're the last ___ house in the neigh - bor - hood to
___ too soon. ___

take down your lights like you should? You're the last ___ house

To Coda ⊕

to take down your lights.

⊕ *Coda*

to take down your ___ lights. _____ But

who am I to say you left them on too late? ___ Who ___ am I to say that you pro-

cras - ti - nate? May - be you're ___ the first _____ to put 'em up, ___

___ or the last house ___ to take 'em down. _____

play 3 times

The last house. ___

37

O Christmas Tree
(O Tannenbaum)

FIRST NOTE

German Folk Melody

1. O Christ - mas Tree! O Christ - mas Tree, you
2. O Christ - mas Tree! O Christ - mas Tree, you much
3. O Christ - mas Tree! O Christ - mas Tree, thy

stand in ver - dant beau - ty! O Christ - mas Tree, O
plea - sure doth thou bring me! O Christ - mas Tree, O
can - dles shine out bright - ly! O Christ - mas Tree, O

Christ - mas Tree, you stand in ver - dant beau - ty! Your boughs are green in
Christ - mas Tree, much plea - sure doth thou bring me! For ev' - ry year, the
Christ - mas Tree, thy can - dles shine out bright - ly! Each bough doth hold its

sum - mer's glow, and do not fade in win - ter's snow. O
Christ - mas Tree brings to us all both joy and glee. O
ti - ny light that makes each toy to spar - kle bright. O

Christ - mas Tree, O Christ - mas Tree, you stand in ver - dant beau - ty!
Christ - mas Tree, O Christ - mas Tree, much plea - sure doth thou bring me!
Christ - mas Tree, O Christ - mas Tree, thy can - dles shine out bright - ly!

O Come, All Ye Faithful
(Adeste Fideles)

Words by
JOHN FRANCIS WADE
Translation by
FREDERICK OAKELEY

Music by
JOHN READING

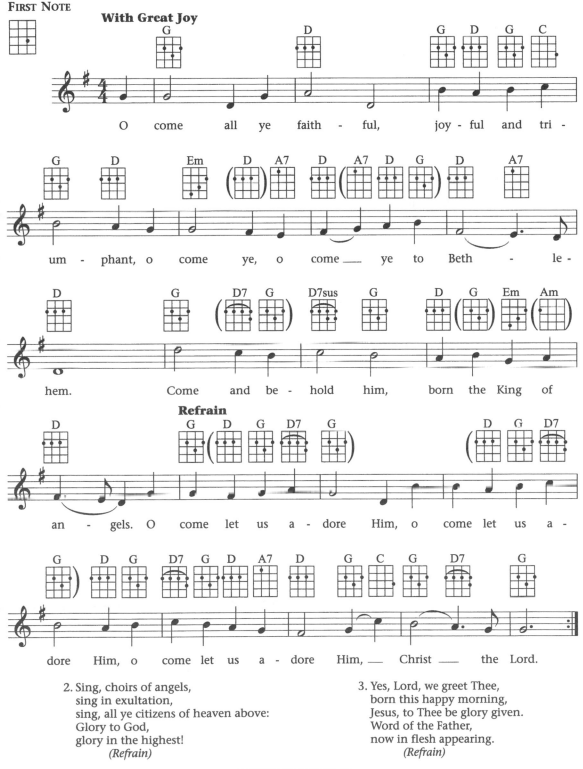

2. Sing, choirs of angels,
   sing in exultation,
   sing, all ye citizens of heaven above:
   Glory to God,
   glory in the highest!
   (Refrain)

3. Yes, Lord, we greet Thee,
   born this happy morning,
   Jesus, to Thee be glory given.
   Word of the Father,
   now in flesh appearing.
   (Refrain)

O Come, O Come Emmanuel

English Translation by
JOHN MASON NEALE

Thirteenth-Century
Latin Melody

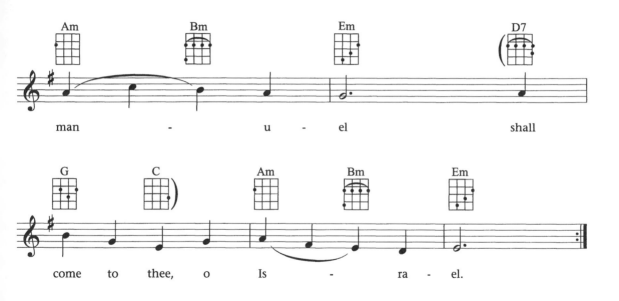

man - u - el shall

come to thee, o Is - ra - el.

3. O come, Thou Day-Spring from on high,
   our spirits by thy drawing nigh,
   disperse the gloomy clouds of night,
   and Death's dark shadows put to flight.
   (Chorus)

4. O come, Thou Key of David, come,
   and open wide our heav'nly home.
   Make safe the way that leads on high,
   and close the path to misery.
   (Chorus)

5. O come, o come, Thou Lord of might,
   who to Thy tribes, on Sinai's height
   in ancient times did'st give the law,
   in cloud and majesty and awe.
   (Chorus)

Christmas Greetings

O Little Town of Bethlehem

Words by
PHILLIPS BROOKS

Music by
LEWIS H. REDNER

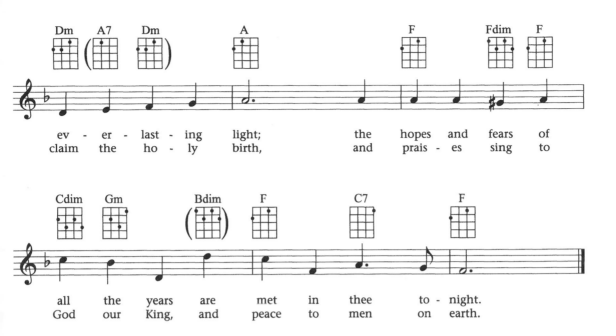

| Dm | A7 | Dm | | A | | | F | | Fdim | F |

ev - er - last - ing light; the hopes and fears of
claim the ho - ly birth, and prais - es sing to

| Cdim | Gm | | Bdim | F | | C7 | | F |

all the years are met in thee to - night.
God our King, and peace to men on earth.

3. How silently, how silently
   the wondrous gift is giv'n!
   So God imparts to human hearts
   the blessings of His heav'n.
   No ear may hear His coming;
   but in this world of sin,
   where meek souls will receive Him still,
   the dear Christ enters in.

4. O Holy Child of Bethlehem
   descent to us, we pray;
   cut out our sin and enter in,
   be born in us today.
   We hear the Christmas angels,
   the great glad tidings tell;
   oh, come to us, abide with us,
   our Lord Emmanuel.

Christmas Greetings

Rise Up, Shepherd, and Follow

Spiritual

leave your ewes and leave your rams, rise up, shep-herd and

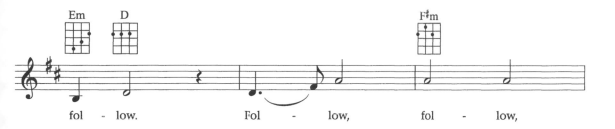

fol - low. Fol - low, fol - low,

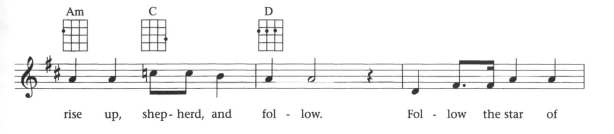

rise up, shep-herd, and fol - low. Fol - low the star of

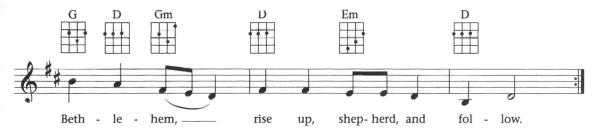

Beth - le - hem, ——— rise up, shep-herd, and fol - low.

A JOYOUS CHRISTMAS

Silent Night

Words by
JOSEPH MÖHR

Music by
FRANZ X. GRUBER

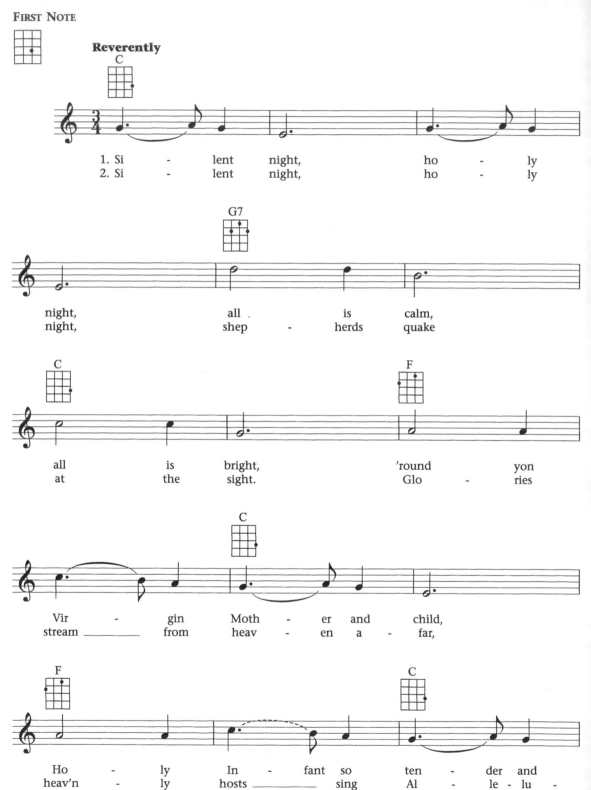

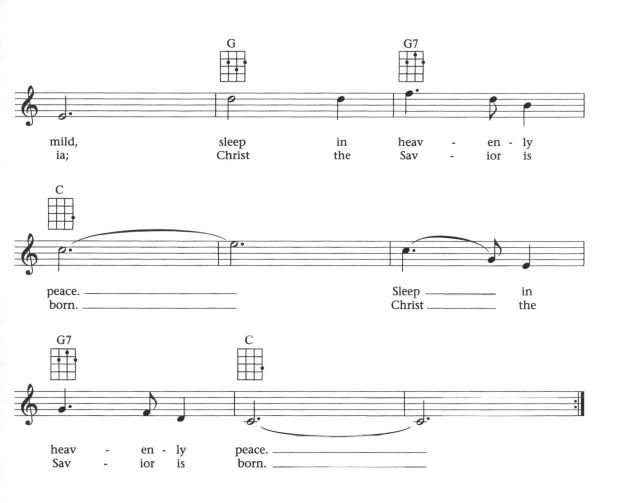

G

G7

mild,   sleep   in   heav - en - ly
ia;   Christ   the   Sav - ior   is

C

peace. _____
born. _____   Sleep _____ in
                                                                                    Christ _____ the

G7   **C**

heav - en - ly   peace. _____
Sav - ior   is   born. _____

3. Silent night, Holy night,
    Son of God, love's pure light.
    Radiant beams from Thy holy face,
    with the dawn of redeeming grace,
    Jesus, Lord, at Thy birth,
    Jesus, Lord, at Thy birth.

The Twelve Days of Christmas

English Traditional Carol

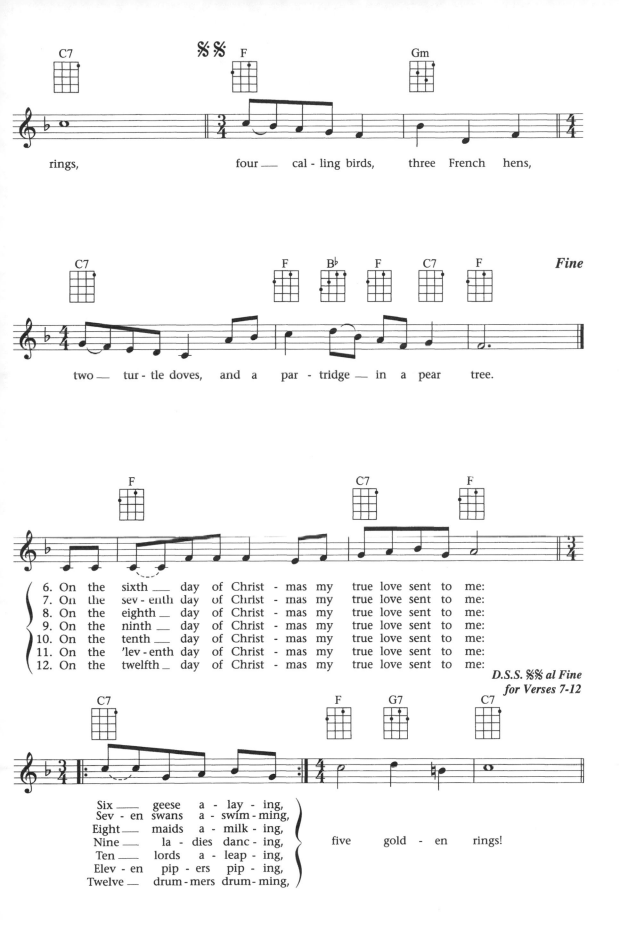

rings, four — cal - ling birds, three French hens,

two — tur - tle doves, and a par - tridge — in a pear tree.

Fine

6. On the sixth __ day of Christ - mas my true love sent to me:
7. On the sev - enth day of Christ - mas my true love sent to me:
8. On the eighth __ day of Christ - mas my true love sent to me:
9. On the ninth __ day of Christ - mas my true love sent to me:
10. On the tenth __ day of Christ - mas my true love sent to me:
11. On the 'lev - enth day of Christ - mas my true love sent to me:
12. On the twelfth __ day of Christ - mas my true love sent to me:

D.S.S. ‰‰ al Fine
for Verses 7-12

Six __ geese a - lay - ing,
Sev - en swans a - swim - ming,
Eight __ maids a - milk - ing,
Nine __ la - dies danc - ing,
Ten __ lords a - leap - ing,
Elev - en pip - ers pip - ing,
Twelve __ drum - mers drum - ming,

five gold - en rings!

We Three Kings of Orient Are

Words & Music by
JOHN HENRY HOPKINS, JR.

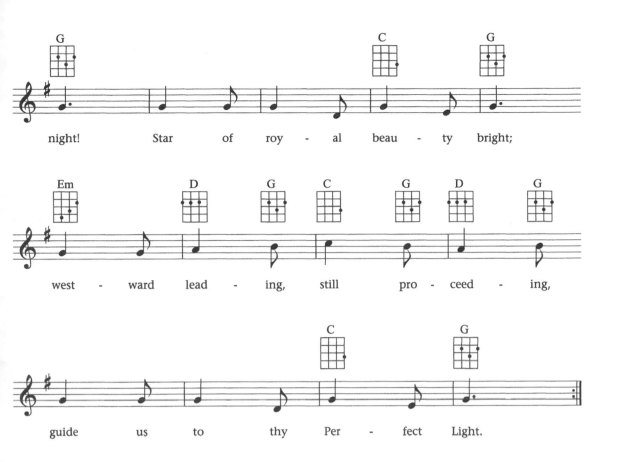

night!   Star   of   roy - al   beau - ty   bright;

west - ward   lead - ing,   still   pro - ceed - ing,

guide   us   to   thy   Per - fect   Light.

3. Frankincense to offer have I,
   incense owns a Deity nigh;
   prayer and praising, all men raising,
   worship Him, God most high.
   (Chorus)

4. Myrrh is mine; its bitter perfume
   breathes a life of gathering gloom;
   sorrowing, sighing, bleeding, dying,
   sealed in the stone cold tomb.
   (Chorus)

5. Glorious now behold Him arise.
   King and God, and sacrifice,
   heaven sings Hallelujah;
   Hallelujah the earth replies.
   (Chorus)

Christmas Remembrance
Shone a heavenly star
     so bright.
Which for Wise Men
     led the way
To the place where
     Jesus lay.

What Child Is This?

Words by
WILLIAM CHATTERTON DIX

English Traditional Melody
Based on "Greensleeves"

FIRST NOTE

Tenderly

What Child   is   this, ——— who   laid   to
Why   lies   He   in ——— such   mean   es -

rest, ——— on   Mar - y's   lap ——— is   sleep -
tate, ——— where   ox   and   ass ——— are   feed -

ing?   Whom   an - gels   greet ——— with   an - thems
ing?   Good   Chris - tian,   fear, ——— for   sin - ners

sweet, ——— while   shep - herds   watch ——— are   keep -
here ——— the   si - lent   Word ——— is   plead -

ing?   This,   this ——— is   Christ   the
ing?   Nails,   spear, ——— shall   pierce   Him

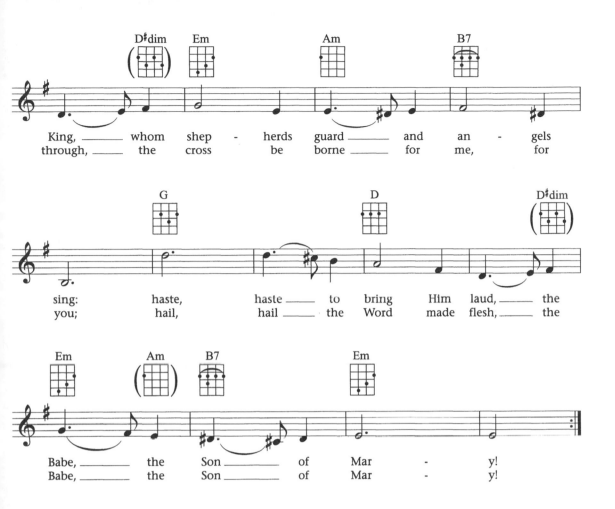

King, _____ whom shep - herds guard _____ and an - gels
through, _____ the cross be borne _____ for me, for

sing: haste, haste _____ to bring Him laud, _____ the
you; hail, hail _____ the Word made flesh, _____ the

Babe, _____ the Son _____ of Mar - y!
Babe, _____ the Son _____ of Mar - y!

3. So bring Him incense, gold and myrrh,
come peasant, king, to own Him.
The King of kings salvation brings,
let loving hearts enthrone Him.
Raise, raise the song on high,
the Virgin sings her lullaby;
joy, joy for Chirst is born,
the Babe, the Son of Mary!

When You're Born on Christmas Day

Music & Lyrics by
JIM BELOFF

FIRST NOTE

1. When you're born —— on Christ - mas day —— they say —— you're
—— 2. on New Year's Eve —— there's dou - ble
3. *Instrumental*

cheat - ed.   That you on - ly get your pres - ents once —— a year.
bub - bly.   When you're born —— on Val - en - tine's —— it's ex - tra sweet.

——   And you nev - er get twice as much, ——   you get
——   And if Hal - lo - ween is your scene, ——   well, the

lost in all —— the hol - i - day cheer.   When you're born——
2. trick is that you
3. *Instrumental*

get twice the treat. ——   And if you de - buted on In - de -
3. And though an - y day's a fine one

54

pend - ence Day, you get a spe - cial kick ___ out of the fi - re -
to ar - rive, I'll tell you why I like ___ the day De - cem - ber

works dis - play. __ *Instrumental*
twen - ty - five. __ When you're born on Christ - mas Day __ you're born with mu -

sic. All __ that mu - sic seems to fill __ the at - mo - sphere, _

__ and that's why I say Christ - mas Day

is the best birth - day, the best birth - day, the

best birth - day of the year. _____

We Wish You a Merry Christmas

English Traditional Carol

1. We wish you a mer-ry Christ-mas, we
2. Now bring us some fig-gy pud-ding, now
3. We won't go un-til we get some, we

wish you a mer-ry Christ-mas, we wish you a mer-ry
bring us some fig-gy pud-ding, now bring us some fig-gy
won't go un-til we get some, now won't go un-til we

Christ-mas, and a hap-py New Year. ⎫
pud-ding and __ bring some right here. ⎬ Good
get some, so __ bring some right here. ⎭

tid-ings we bring for you and your kin. We

wish you a mer-ry Christ-mas, and a hap-py New Year.